Snakes on the Hunt
COBRAS

Dennis Rudenko

PowerKiDS
press

New York

Published in 2017 by The Rosen Publishing Group, Inc.
29 East 21st Street, New York, NY 10010

First Edition

Editor: Caitie McAneney
Book Design: Mickey Harmon

Photo Credits: Cover, pp. 1, 4, 6, 8, 10, 18 (series logo) iLoveCoffeeDesign/Shutterstock.com; cover, pp. 1, 3, 4, 6, 8, 10, 12, 14, 16, 18, 20, 22—24 (background) cla78/Shutterstock.com; cover (cobra) Heinrich van den Berg/Gallo Images/Getty Images; p. 5 Andre Coetzer/Shutterstock.com; pp. 7 (inset), 13 CraigBurrows/Shutterstock.com; pp. 7 (main), 15 Heiko Kiera/Shutterstock.com; p. 9 AFP/Stringer/AFP/Getty Images; p. 11 BENZINE/Shutterstock.com; p. 17 (main) Suriya99/Shutterstock.com; p. 17 (inset) Ekkachai/Shutterstock.com; p. 19 stuportsshut21/Shutterstock.com; p. 21 Angelo Giampiccolo/Shutterstock.com; p. 22 Matthew Cole/Shutterstock.com.

Cataloging-in-Publication Data

Names: Rudenko, Dennis.
Title: Cobras / Dennis Rudenko.
Description: New York : PowerKids Press, 2017. | Series: Snakes on the hunt | Includes index.
Identifiers: ISBN 9781499421941 (pbk.) | ISBN 9781499421965 (library bound) | ISBN 9781499421958 (6 pack)
Subjects: LCSH: Cobras–Juvenile literature.
Classification: LCC QL666.O64 R83 2017| DDC 597.96–dc23

Manufactured in the United States of America

CPSIA Compliance Information: Batch #BS16PK: For Further Information contact Rosen Publishing, New York, New York at 1-800-237-9932

Contents

A Quiver of Cobras

What could be scarier than a snake that can stand? Cobras are great hunters with supersenses. They are very **venomous**, and they use their bite to kill **prey**.

There are about 270 different snakes called cobras. However, there are only around 20 "true" cobras in the world. They include the forest cobra and Ashe's spitting cobra. Other snakes, like the king cobra, share the name, but not the **genus**. They still have many features similar to those of true cobras.

Snake Bites

A group of cobras is called a quiver.

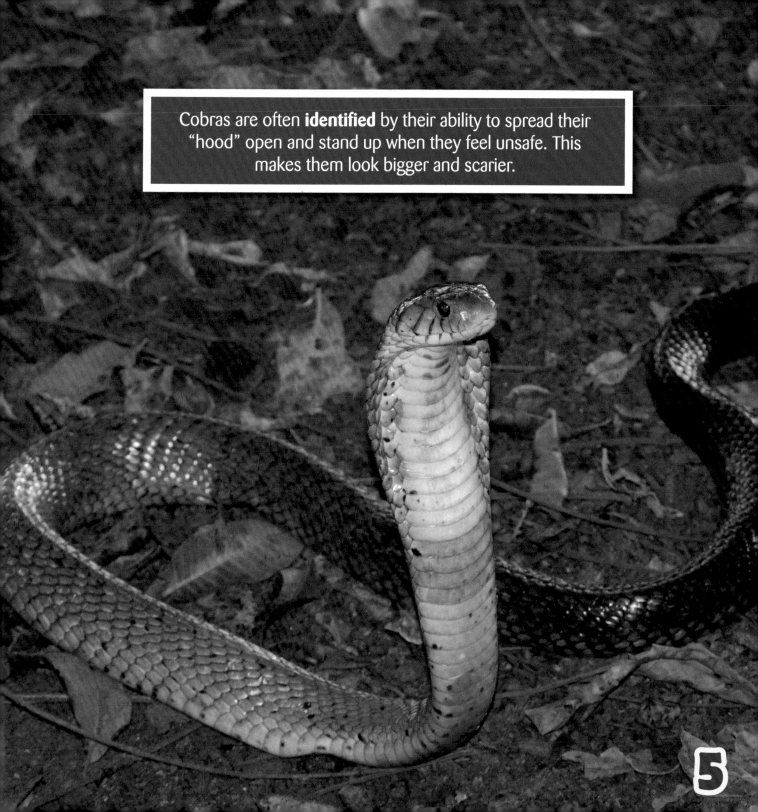

Cobras are often **identified** by their ability to spread their "hood" open and stand up when they feel unsafe. This makes them look bigger and scarier.

Identifying a Cobra

How can you identify a cobra if you see one? Look at its features. Most cobras can spread out the ribs in their neck to create a flat hood. Cobras come in many colors, such as black, yellow, white, brown, and red. Many cobras have patterns on their skin, such as circles and stripes. Like most snakes, they have smooth scales.

Cobras kill their prey with venom, which they **inject** from two long teeth called fangs. The fangs pierce the skin of the cobra's prey and deliver deadly venom.

Snake Bites

Some cobras grow to huge lengths. The forest cobra is the longest true cobra, reaching 10 feet (3 m). The king cobra can grow up to 18 feet (5.5 m) long!

Indian cobra

king cobra

The Indian cobra is also called the spectacled cobra. That's because the marking on its hood looks almost like spectacles, or glasses.

Life of a Cobra

Like many snakes, most cobras start out in eggs. A king cobra can lay between 20 and 40 eggs at a time. It takes over two months for babies to break out of their shells. During that time, the mother cobra guards her eggs. There are a few predators who would love to grab one!

The king cobra is the only snake that makes a nest. The mother cobra moves her body around to collect leaves, which she uses to cover her eggs. Then she lies on her eggs to keep them safe.

Snake Bites

Baby cobras have venom, too! They are just as deadly as their parents.

Baby cobras are ready to take care of themselves soon after they're born.

Cobra Habitats

Cobras live in many different **habitats**. They're found in India, Southeast Asia, Indonesia, the Middle East, and Africa. Their colors and patterns may be different depending on their **region**.

Many cobras like to live in tropical forests, which are hot and wet. They can climb trees! Others like to slither along the ground in grasslands. Sometimes they sneak onto farms to hunt. Cobras can even be found swimming through the water! Like most snakes, they're very good swimmers.

Snake Bites

Those who follow the Hindu religion consider cobras to be godlike. Cobras are connected with the god Shiva.

China

India

king cobra area

Many cobras are solitary, which means they like to live alone.

Cobra Supersenses

Cobras have special senses that make them master hunters. They have good eyesight, especially at night. They have a special body part called a Jacobson's **organ** on the roof of their mouth. A cobra's tongue collects a smell and then sends it to the Jacobson's organ, which recognizes the smell.

Cobras can sense **vibrations** on the ground. This helps them know when prey or predators are nearby. Cobras can even sense changes in temperature around them. Nothing can get past a cobra!

A cobra's senses make it an unstoppable hunter.

13

Cobra Defenses

Not many animals will mess with a cobra. You don't even want to get close! However, the cobra has also developed **defenses** that keep predators and people away.

If a cobra feels unsafe, it may raise the upper part of its body off the ground. Large cobras can stand as tall as a person! The cobra spreads its neck ribs so its hood flattens out. The hood makes it look bigger to other animals. Then, the snake will hiss.

The hiss of a king cobra is so deep and loud it can sound like a dog's growl.

15

A Cobra's Favorite Foods

Cobras will eat almost anything they can find, catch, and swallow. Some even eat their own kind. This makes them cannibals. They also eat other kinds of snakes, especially smaller ones.

Cobras also hunt lizards, birds, and eggs. They're known to eat small **mammals**, such as mice. If a cobra comes across a dead animal, it might eat that as well. Cobras take a long time to **digest** their food. This means they can go weeks or even months without eating.

Cobras aren't picky eaters. They'll take what they can get!

On the Hunt!

Most cobras hunt early or late in the day. When they find a meal, they strike very quickly to take their prey by surprise. Cobras then deliver a venomous bite with their sharp fangs.

A bite from a cobra is enough to kill a large animal, such as an elephant. While their venom isn't as strong as that of some snakes, cobras deliver a large amount of venom. A king cobra's bite has enough venom to kill 20 people!

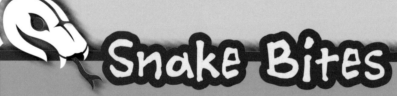

Snake Bites

Most animals die if they're bitten by a cobra. However, if a person is bitten, they can take a special drug called antivenin. This stops the effects of venom.

Some cobras can spray venom, but this trick is usually used on enemies, not prey. This is a Mozambique spitting cobra.

Cobras at Risk

Cobras are at the top of their food chain. However, that doesn't mean they're completely safe from predators. Other cobras and snakes hunt smaller cobras. Small mammals called mongooses can kill cobras. That's because mongooses have thick coats that fangs have trouble piercing. They're also very fast and can avoid the cobra's bite.

People are the greatest risk to cobras, though. They cut down the cobras' forest homes. People in India catch cobras and use them in illegal snake charming.

Snake charmers play an instrument so that it seems as if the snake is "dancing" to it. Most snake charmers remove the cobra's fangs, which harms the cobra.

21

Keeping Cobras Safe

There's no hunter like a cobra! With their great defenses and supersenses, cobras are the top hunters in their habitats. Some people disagree about which cobras are true cobras and which ones aren't. However, many snakes share the ability to spread their hoods, stand up, and strike.

Whether a cobra is "true" or not, it should be treated with care. Cobras need their habitats to be saved for years to come. These awesome animals need space to live and hunt!

Glossary

defense: A feature of a living thing that helps keep it safe.

digest: To break down food inside the body so that the body can use it.

genus: The scientific name for a group of plants or animals that share many features. It includes a larger group of animals than just one species.

habitat: The natural place where an animal or plant lives.

identify: To tell what something is.

inject: To force something into the body using a needle or sharp teeth.

mammal: A warm-blooded animal that has a backbone and hair, breathes air, and feeds milk to its young.

organ: A body part that does a certain task.

prey: An animal hunted by other animals for food.

region: A large area of land that has a number of features in common.

venomous: Having a poisonous bite or sting.

vibration: Small, quick, back-and-forth movements.

Index

Websites

Due to the changing nature of Internet links, PowerKids Press has developed an online list of websites related to the subject of this book. This site is updated regularly. Please use this link to access the list: www.powerkidslinks.com/soth/cobra